MW00639614

# EXPLORING NATURE THROUGH POETRY

PERCY E. MILLS

ISBN 978-1-0980-4051-2 (hardcover)
ISBN 978-1-0980-4053-6 (digital)

Christian Faith Publishing, Inc.
832 Park Avenue
Meadville, PA 16335
www.christianfaithpublishing.com

Printed in the United States of America

This book is dedicated to those I admire with regard to their devotion and appreciation for the beautiful environment in which we live—from a small laborer that is trying to introduce nature to its parasitic dwellers.

# Contents

"When I consider thy heavens, the work of thy fingers, the moon and the stars, which thou hast ordained; What is man, that thou art mindful of him? and the son of man, that thou visitest him?" Psalm 8:3–4 KJV

I acknowledge

…God, the Creator of all, for generously supplying our every need

…Our family and loved ones who have been so supportive

…Our CFP family whose tireless and diligent efforts made this book possible

Credits

Dilemma artwork by Eric E. Mills
Inquiry artwork by Aaron A. Mills
Hummingbirds by Nancy LeJune

# Conscious Unawareness

Many have looked,
But few have seen
The swirling patterns created by
The rocks that lie in a stream.

Several have taken temporary shelter
From the falling rain,
But did not hear the concert given
By the queen of musical fame.

There are those who rise
With the dawn's early light,
But miss the songs the birds sing
Before they take their flight.

Others have stood at the foot of a mountain
Covered with huge boulders of stone,
But overlooked an art collection
Larger than anyone could ever own.

If you have not the patience
To diligently seek,
On the depth of nature
You cannot speak.

# Mystical Clouds

Fluffy clusters of clouds
Slowly drifting by
A bright, silvery moon
High up in the sky.

Oh, what beauty
And elegant grace,
With silent visual rhythm
The wind sets the pace.

Taunting the imagination
With stunning works of art
That swiftly come together
And slowly drift apart.

Accented and highlighted
By the moon's metallic light,
Each majestic figure
Is radiantly brought to life.

Every cloud formation
Reveals thoughts of the inner mind;
For each observer sees it differently
Although viewed at the same time.

One sees a ferocious lion,
Another, a dancing bear;
And the third, a beautiful maiden
With long flowing hair.

This strange phenomenon,
Many have tried to explain,
Is only one of nature's wild mysteries
That man will never tame.

# *Mystery and Honor*

Sufficient light
Is the perfect aid to sight,
And cautious is the mind
When darkness rules the time.

But between the dark and daylight
Lies a mystifying space,
When neither dark nor daylight
Has actually taken place.

Concealing recognition,
Defying colors hue;
Distorting height and distance,
Impairing judgment, too.

One who dares to tread
During this deceptive time,
May even be deceived
By imaginations of the mind.

The playing of a national anthem,
The raising of a flag,
Standing in quiet honor
Is something man has always had.

What then is the mystery
That lies between the dark and light?
It's only nature's way
Of keeping honor right.

And who deserves more honor
Than He who raises the flag
That covers the whole universe
Without a wrinkle or sag.

Out of the Precepts
of a Man's Own Mind
Proceeds Forth
The Very Things
that Condemns His Own Soul

# The Amazing Universe

When it's dark
And the sky is clear,
Observe the universe
The planets seem so near.

Meditate
Or just relax your mind,
You'll soon wonder, as man has
Since the dawn of time.

Look at the moon
All that beauty and grace,
Can you imagine
How it was hung in place?

A star that's been suspended
For eons of time
Is released
Leaving a fiery trail behind.

Racing across
The atmosphere,
Creating mixed emotions
Of excitement and fear.

Abruptly
Just as it appeared
The star disintegrates
The fire disappears.

Captivated by
The astonishing space
You begin to imagine,
Your eyes start to trace.

Recognizing the image of a character
Whose stories you have read,
The imagination and images
Drastically spread.

The sky becomes
A lighted drawing space
With imaginary lines
That you create.

After tracing images
Around the galaxy
You finally realize
The true reality.

The stars and planets throughout
The whole universe
Are scribed
In perfect pictorial verse.

When it Comes to Heaven,
If you want to be a "No Show,"
Then Just Go With the Flow

# Nature in Concert

Nature slowly pulls her blind
At the end of a bright, hot summer day;
Birds swiftly gather in their roosting place
After hours of feeding and play.

Chirping argumentatively
In the mighty press,
They nudge for position
Then silently take their rest.

The light ceremoniously
Relinquishes its command;
A warm blanket of darkness
Covers the water and land.

Dots, dits, and dashes
Gracefully embrace the night
With greenish glowing
Intermittent flashes of light.

Fireflies are the main attraction
At nature's outdoor ballet;
The temperature sets the tempo
As cricket violinists play.

The barn owl joins in
Hooting a mellow baritone sound,
While katydids add stereo wood blocks
From positions all around.

The bullfrog croaks
A big, deep bass
That echoes off the water and
Can be heard all over the place.

So the next time
It's a hot summer night
And sleeping conditions
Just aren't right…

Take a drive to the country,
Park near a river, pond, or lake;
Watch and listen to the beauty
Creatures of nature can make.

# *Closing the Gap*

In the midst of the forest
Below the many trees,
Lying almost level
Are the late fall leaves.

Walk briskly
Along your way;
Moving quietly is almost an impossibility
On a late fall day.

Come take a seat
On that old fallen tree;
And watch the furry little animals
On their fall shopping spree.

Now you mind
They're all aware;
They heard you coming
And they know you're there.

Some hid themselves
Beneath the leaves;
While others are clinging
To the backside of the trees.

They will hold their position
*Until* you let them know
That you're a friendly visitor
And not a foe.

This is a crucial moment,
And one you must not lose;
Deciding whether they stay or leave
Is something they must choose.

Sit as still
As you can possibly be,
And don't become physically excited
Over the first animal you see.

Any sudden move
Or loud outburst
Will cause all the little animals
To disperse.

The squirrels will ascend
To the top of the trees
And duck in their holes
To a soft bed of leaves.

The chipmunks will retreat
Beneath the ground,
And they'll all find another shopping place
Where you're not around.

Now everything
Is going just swell;
You've been watching the little animals
For quite a spell.

They've become accustomed
To your presence there,
And are once again collecting
Food from everywhere.

They're even collecting acorns
From around your feet,
Why don't you share that bag of peanuts
You brought along to eat?

Open the bag quietly
And place a few nuts on the tree
In a nice, clear spot
Where they can easily see.

Come and visit
About the same time every day,
And make all of your movements slowly
So you won't scare the animals away.

With a little time and patience
You'll accomplish something not many can;
You'll have a lot of friendly wild animals
Eating peanuts from your hand.

*Receive the Highest*
*Yield Ever Paid*
*Invest in the Lord*

# *Dual Inspiration*

Labor,
But not for profit alone;
Strive for perfection
And satisfaction of your own.

No matter how great
Or small the task may be,
The manner of accomplishment
Is oh so important you see.

The task at hand is only a small but intricate
Part of the ongoing, interlocking system
Propelled by the passing of time;
Not only accomplishing the task,
But conditioning the discipline of the mind.

# *Defiant Voyager*

Unassisted by artificial light
Or apparatus to supply me with air,
I have plunged to the floor of the ocean
And explored the mysteries there.

Visited the planets that glimmer
With subdued stroboscopical-colored light,
Making the incredible journey
Beyond the speed of sight.

Surveyed the scorching surface
Of the hottest star, the sun,
I have even found the Garden of Eden
Where little work was ever done.

These are but a few of the things
I have accomplished with the passing of time,
Merely by entering the
Unlimited imagination of the mind.

# *Dilemma*

If it were
Mere rope or twine,
Wherewith
Your snare doth bind.

The burning passion
I have for you
Would burn wherewith
You hold me through.

'Tis not a combustible
That holds me fast,
But chains that were molten
When they were cast.

Now tempered and cold
They tightly bind
Me and the others
You left behind.

My burning passion
Doth still brightly glow,
But not hot enough
To make the chains flow.

Howbeit, if our passions
Somehow again could meet,
The chains would melt asunder
In flowing molten, white heat.

In the midst of this tumultuous passion,
Would I have presence of mind
To escape—or remain—
Hoping your love would forever be mine?

# *After the Storm*

The water's calm
Not a cloud in sight,
But the restless spirit within me
Warns that something isn't right.

An eerie stillness surrounds us,
There's not a soul that doesn't know;
The winds are gathered together
For a mighty blow.

Clear the surface of everything
That will stop the waters flow.
Tie down all the cargo
In the decks below.

Batten down all the hatches—
Bring down the sail;
And prepare to face a storm
That will threaten even the mighty whale.

The only one aloft is the
Watchman in the crow's-nest
Keeping a constant vigil to the
North, South, East, and West.

The crew is anxiously awaiting
The watchman's final sign,
So the ship can be anchored
Bow first to the storm line.

All the physical preparation
Is finally over and done.
The crew is in the dark hull;
Mental stress and tension have just begun.

The silent, heavy darkness is suddenly pierced
By a loud, deep voice singing a mighty song;
A few listen intently to the words,
While the rest ponder over memories
Of all the things they've ever done wrong.

While the mighty storm is raging
And pounding against the hull,
A lot of personal promises and commitments
Are mentally made by all.

Once again the water finally
Settles to its normal line
Leaving heavy structural damage,
But the crew is fine.

A lot of good intentions
In that dark hull were born,
But now will they be kept
*After* the storm?

# Serene Spirit

The body is a tangible organism
That one can feel,
But the soul is an intangible spirit
Never proven by man to be real.

The skin protects the delicate
Organism that lies beneath,
But the soul is shielded
By one's belief.

Content is the soul that dwells
Within the body of an honest man,
Graciously moving through spacious
Chambers and corridor undaunted
Vigorously thriving on radiant atmosphere
Generated by kind thought and deed.

There are no doors separating
The chambers from the corridor,
Nor is there any need,
For this soul dwells alone.

# *Inquiry*

O death, hast not one mortal
Stayed your icy hand?
Out of all those who lie victim,
Hast not one possessed the key?

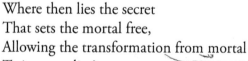

Mortals have pierced the depth of the earth
And taken treasures from within,
Defied the bonds of gravity and soared aloft
Yet still remain prisoners of mortality.

Where then lies the secret
That sets the mortal free,
Allowing the transformation from mortal
To immortality?

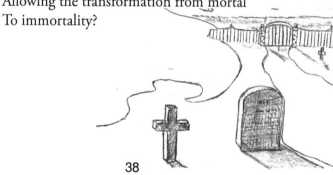

# Young Tree

A fairly young tree said to an older tree
On a windy summer day.
"I hope this terrible wind
Doesn't blow my leaves away."

Then he braced himself
And leaned the other way.
The older tree shouted quickly,
"You'll lose a limb that way.

"Just relax and let yourself sway
And let your branches dance and play.
You may lose a leaf or two
But that's something we all do.

"Besides in the autumn
They'll all fall down
And our leaves will be scattered
All over the ground.

"But that's no reason
To shed a tear,
Because in the spring
They'll all reappear."

# Spring

Feel the soothing warmth
Of the morning sun;
See the pretty trees
New life has just begun.

Smell the sweet fragrance
Of the blossoms they bear;
Beautiful little flowers
Are blooming everywhere.

Crystal clear water
Has filled the little brooks;
Green grass has covered the valleys
How magnificent it all looks.

Birds are singing
Their lovely songs of cheer;
Tender hearts are beating
In creatures everywhere.

Oh, thank God
It's spring once again,
A true sign that God's tender mercy
Still dwells on earth with men.

# *Graceful Reminder*

A long neck that's
Part of a straight line
Extending from the bill to the
Two web feet that trail behind.

Long wide wings
That catch a lot of air
To lift the heavy body
That they must bear.

Flying in a precise formation
That forms a long, wide "V",
Watching the Canadian geese in flight
Is a rewarding sight to see.

Trumpeting
As they go,
Attracting the attention
Of all those below.

Making a statement,
Signing the victory
Of peace and how good
It is to be free.

# Trainquillity

*"The calmnest one derives from listening to the sounds of a passing train"*

In the far distance
Is a faint but familiar sound
Of a train locomotive
That doesn't seem to be covering much ground

The sound
Will gradually intensify
'Til the train's locomotive
Has passed by.

Then clickity clack,
Clickity clack,
The sound of the train wheels
Passing over the rail crack.

The soothing rhythm
Is like a hypnotic spell,
Drawing your mind into a fantasy
Of that of a fairy tale.

Where the train came from
And where it's headed for,
All the possibilities
You begin to explore.

Rumbling of the train cars
And the periodic tinkling of the bell
Greatly enhances
The mystifying spell.

Visualizing all the beautiful cities, mountains
And valleys the train has passed through;
Crossing rivers and flat lands
Even the desert, too.

The sound diminishes
And is about to cease,
When the train whistle blows
Leaving a lingering feeling of peace.

If you live in one of the small towns
That the train passes through,
It will greatly increase your imagination
And aid your sleeping, too.

There is no other land transportation
With such a luring beckon call.
When it comes to the locomotive, it's the most
Mesmerizing and *grand* father of them all.

# Things with Wings

In a large opening
Between the small branches of a tree
A spider constructs a web
That is very hard to see.

Attaching straight strands
From the outer perimeter,
Which are all connected
In the center.

The strands are much closer, but
Resembling spokes of an old wagon wheel,
With precise spacing
Revealing the spider's skill.

Forming a large circle
On the outer perimeter;
Repeating the process with progressively
Smaller circles 'til they reach the center.

Duplicating the same spacing
Used in the straight strands,
Forming an intricate pattern of
A fine doily made by skillful hands.

After completing
His skillful feat
The spider does a transformation
That is awfully neat.

Folding his legs
Like a magical trick
He then appears
As an old, dry stick.

Patiently waiting
Calm and still
For any disturbance in the web
He could easily feel.

The first victim
Is a little old gnat
Barely disturbing the web
Which remained still and flat.

The spider calmly remains
In his disguise
Knowing the gnat
Wasn't a very good prize.

The spider didn't have
To wait very long
Before a fly got caught
And he was big and strong.

Shaking
The web all about,
Rapidly moving his wings
And trying to get out.

The spider quickly
Went to his aid,
Wrapped him in a sticky coat of webbing
And dinner was made.

# *Wind*

Heard, felt,
But not seen.
Fast, slow,
Or perfectly serene.

Fanning the flames
Of a forest fire,
Aiding and abetting
Its disintegrating power.

A raging typhoon that
Causes the ocean to overflow;
The devastating hurricane
Or a destructive tornado.

Flags and banners
Wave when it's near,
Displaying symbols of countries
And things we hold dear.

Large windmills
Turning briskly,
Moving by its power
Producing clean electricity.

Hot air balloons float
Gracefully across the sky
Covered with logos and beautiful colors
As it's passing by.

A welcome relief
On a hot summer day,
Passing through water fountains
Causing a misty spray.

Birds and gliders
Assisted in their flight;
Large ships with sails
Driven by its might.

Tall grass, fields of wheat,
And the leafy tree,
All bow
To its majesty.

Always a friend and sometimes
Thought of as a foe;
But everything it does has a purpose,
The reason, we don't always know.

# Hummingbird

Small, with jewel-like colors
Brilliant in the sun;
Swift, feisty, and maneuverability
That fascinates everyone.

Rapidly vibrating wings
Producing a humming sound;
Giving it the speed
To cover a lot of ground.

Almost like magic
It can suddenly appear,
Attracted by flowers and trees
That are blooming anywhere.

Flying side to side, forward, backward,
EVEN up and down;
Or hovering while sipping nectar through
A long, slender bill—whenever it is found.

Pollinating the flowers
Of a bush, plant, or tree;
Aiding their shape and color
Throughout its territory.

One of nature's crown jewels
As anyone can see,
Not only possessing beauty,
But causing it to be.

There's no Grease on
The Road to Heaven
So You Can't Just Slide In

# Oak Data

That old oak tree has been
Standing there for quite a while;
And if it could talk, a lot of
Interesting stories it would tell.

Overheard sweet verses being
Whispered in a lover's ear
Filled with emotion
And completely sincere.

Its large leaves were protection
From the scorching sun
For a weary traveler verbally reasoning
How changes in his life could be done.

Those two rings perfectly spaced
On that strong limb way up there
Were probably made by a child's swing
Years ago when it was way down here.

Nursery rhymes and fantasies recited
With the rhythm of the swing
Wishes for special gifts that
Holidays and birthdays would bring.

Spelling and time tables
Were repeated constantly,
Preparing young minds to assist
In what their future would be.

Birds sang beautiful songs
While perched up in those branches;
Steps, music, rhythm
And a lot of ethnic dances.

Prayers for soldiers
Who were away at war;
Weddings, games,
And a whole lot more.

That old tree has an archive
Of history, deep within,
That can only be retrieved through the
Imagination and clues upon its skin.

# Detested Pest

We can all understand
The busy honeybee
Collecting pollen
From the flower or a tree.

With a little bit of reason
We can even justify
The plight of a rodent
Or the pesty little fly.

But there's one winged insect
That's a hypodermic syringe
Who flies around sucking blood
Leaving bumps and itchy skin.

Hatched on stagnant water
In the stump of a hollow tree
Or backed up sewer water
That is rank as it can be.

I'd rather be stuck
By a thorn or a thistle;
I can even take the pain
Of a hypodermic pistol.

But there's one thing
I just can't see
A filthy old mosquito
Sucking blood out of me.

Make Your Reservations
In Advance
There'll be
no Party Crashers
in Heaven

# "Operation Empathy"

I was seated in a room with about thirty fellow police officers each of whom were about to complete a course in Middle Management. Today's assignment had been clearly spelled out in black and white. The document stated no one would be wearing the "uniform of the day" when reporting to the classroom. Everyone would be dressed in old and shabby clothes that could even have paint splatter on them and shoes with rundown heels, thus portraying a person in destitute circumstances.

The course project was designed to help the line supervisor understand the fundamentals of human behavior.

The events are summed up as follows in "The Degenerate."

# The Degenerate

On the first of May
Nineteen Hundred Sixty-eight,
The pride of a degenerate
I tried to create.

I placed a homemade scar
On the right side of my face,
Just to add a little more
For the general public's distaste.

Laying aside
My own personal view,
I put on some raggedy clothes
And took a look at life anew.

From the eyes
Of a poor and lowly man,
I tried to attain the feelings
Of the people of this land.

I entered the public
Raggedy and disgraced
To see how my appearance
Would take to the human race.

I entered a crowded drugstore
Where people were dressed real fine,
And I walked close by
Where they sit and dine.

An eye or two
Or maybe more
Did gaze upon me
As I crossed the floor.

I dare not think
What some might do
Should I have decided
To sit down and dine, too.

As I left
A thought entered my mind,
Gee, I'm glad I don't
Have to dress this way *all* the time.

And then again thinking as
The poor and lowly man,
I looked up and sighted
A lovely fruit stand.

Knowing just
What he might do,
I stopped and eyed the fruit
Quite sad and blue.

The keeper who
Stood nearby
Looked at me
With sorrow in his eye.

I may have sparked
A little compassion in his heart,
And he didn't seem satisfied
'Til a piece of the fruit he did depart.

I did not realize
What he had done,
Until I reached and caught
The big orange he had flung.

Crossing the street
'Cause of the little pride,
I was not able
To subside.

Approaching three young ladies
Who were coming my way,
I decided to speak
To see what their eyes would say.

The first smiled and looked
Straight at me,
As though she had to do this
To keep her dignity.

The second looked at me
With a smirk on her face,
As though to say
My, what a disgrace!

The third turned her head
So I wouldn't be in her view,
But as soon as I passed
She turned and looked too.

Passing through
A glass swinging door,
I entered a public bank
And strolled 'cross the floor.

People moving hurriedly
And seemingly pressed for time,
I don't guess my appearance
Ever crossed their mind.

Only one neatly-dressed young gentleman
Who kept his eye on me,
And not until I had left the bank
Did his mind seem free.

Entering a little candy shop
I know that the keeper thought
I wouldn't have a penny
To pay for anything I bought.

Looking a little weary
And kind of unsteady on my feet,
I walked out to the sidewalk
Where I took a seat.

It wasn't too long after
I saw the keeper disappear
That two uniform policemen
Were questioning me about my presence there.

I gave them the information
That they requested from me,
And finally I told them
My true identity.

They even seemed reluctant
After seeing my identification,
And one of them insisted
He'd have to check out this information.

After giving them a phone number
As I had been instructed to do,
One of them made a check
And found out that it was true.

Leaving and coming upon
A nice looking hotel,
I sat down in front
Where I could be seen real well.

The manager came out
With a seemingly look of fear
That some of the passersby would think
I was staying there.

I only sat upon his step
A little span of time,
And finally when I did depart
I think he had peace of mind.

While sitting there
On the bottom step
Along came a minister
With a white collar 'round his neck.

And looked at me
With a smile upon his face,
Just as though he knew
In Heaven, even *I* had a little space.

# *Sun*

A large hot sphere
So brilliantly bright
Turns the darkness
Into light.

Cannot be viewed
With naked eyes.
Then clouds turn beautiful
Colors just before its rise.

It's the ruler
Of the day,
Causes sad feelings
To go away.

Melts away
Winter snow,
Helps the trees
And plants to grow.

Provides so many
Of our needs,
Warms the earth
So we can plant our seeds.

Provides light
So work can be done.
Warms water and air
For outdoor fun.

Increases the distance
Eyes can see,
And it's all done
Without a fee.

There's so many things
That it can do.
Here I only
Mention a few.

At the end of the day
It's not over yet.
It lifts our spirits
With a beautiful sunset.

Let us thank God
For the sun,
And all other magnificent
Things He has done.

# *Horizon*

Travel in any direction,
Reach it if you can,
The place where the sky
Meets the water or land.

It may seem close
Or far, far away;
But you'll never reach it
If you travel night and day.

There are things that are possible;
And those that are impossible, too.
Always make wise decisions
So your life will be profitable to you.

# *Time*

Sought after,
Inquired about.
We're under its control
And we'll never get out.

Like a giant wave
It moves us along
From the beginning of life
Until we are gone.

Calculated in years,
Months, weeks, days,
Hours, minutes, seconds,
And much smaller ways.

It's part of
Everything we do,
And how it is used
Is up to you.

There's time for everything
Under the sun,
But it's very important
Why, when, and *how* it is done.

# Grave Dust

Feeling sad,
Just received the news
Grave dust will soon
Be settling on my shoes.

One of my friends
Passed away.
Just talked to him
The other day.

It could have been me.
It could have been you.
And there isn't anything
That we can do.

Be kind to your friends
And family.
You never know
Who the next one will be.

Hug and kiss your little ones
Each and every day,
And remember they're listening
To every word you say.

Teach them good things
That will sustain them in that day
When grave dust settles on their shoes
When *you* pass away.

*Self-Discipline
is The Key
to a Better World*

# Personal Disclosure

There are dreams
Messages from Heaven for the soul.
Some peaceful and relaxing,
Others are meant to scold.

Troubling dreams are warnings
Of what *will* come,
Or to let us know
The sinful deed we have done.

It may be a blessing
For the good you are doing,
But it could be punishment
For the evil we are pursuing.

God sends His messenger
To interpret the dream for you,
Whether good or bad
The interpretation *will* come true.

# *About the Author*

Percy E. Mills taught Bible study and served as a church trustee. He later was honorably discharged from the United States Air Force before joining the Metropolitan Police Department, Washington, DC. With nearly two decades of experience in law enforcement, he did a lot of public speaking on the radio and also at the FBI Academy where he graduated in 1975. He later began compiling and reciting his many poems from memory. His previous work *Jewel of the Night* is a colorfully illustrated poetic composition about the City of Pittsburgh. He and wife, Dianne, have five children, Eric, Aaron, Troy, Deborah, and Cheryl.

CPSIA information can be obtained
at www.ICGtesting.com
Printed in the USA
BVHW021127170821
614006BV00006B/6